SIZERGH CASTLE

Cumbria

National Trust

Sizergh Castle is 3½ miles south of Kendal, signposted off A590

Acknowledgements

The National Trust is indebted to Mrs Thomas Hornyold-Strickland, for her helpful comments on the text of this guidebook, and to all those who have contributed to its production. Particular thanks are due to Dr Edward Corp, who wrote the section on the Strickland family; the late Dr Ian Goodall of English Heritage, York, whose architectural survey of Sizergh Castle reassessed the history of the building; Dr Geoffrey Beard, Dr Claire Gapper, Dr Beryl Lott, Richard Dean and the late Angus Taylor, who generously supplied unpublished information from their research; and Malcolm Hutcheson, Head Gardener at Sizergh for 31 years until his retirement in 2001, who gave invaluable help with the section on the garden.

Photographs: English Heritage / National Monuments Record pp. 6, 7 (top and bottom), 25; Country Life Picture Library p. 29; National Trust / Graham Edwards pp. 5 (top); National Trust Images / Andrew Butler pp. 9, 34, 41; NT Images / Brian and Nina Chapple p. 35; NT Images / Val Corbett front cover pp. 33, 36; NT Images / Andreas von Einsiedel pp. 10, 11, 12 (top), 13, 15, 17, 19, 21, 23 (top), 24, 27, 28; NT Images / John Hammond pp. 1, 5 (bottom), 8, 12 (bottom), 22, 23 (bottom), 26, 42, 43, back cover; Norwyn Photographics pp. 4, 14, 18, 44, 45 (top and bottom), 46 (top and bottom), 47, 48 (top left and right and bottom), 49 (left and right), 50, 51 (top left and right and bottom), 52, 53, 54 (left and right), 55 (left and right), 56 (left and right).

Bird's-eye view of the garden by Eric Thomas
© 2001 The National Trust
Registered charity no. 205846
ISBN 978-1-84359-301-0
Reprinted 2008, 2011; revised 2007, 2009, 2010
If you would like to become a member or make a donation, please telephone 0844 800 1895 (minicom 0844 800 4410); write to The National Trust, PO Box 39, Warrington WA5 7WD; or see our website at www.nationaltrust.org.uk
Typeset from disc and designed by James Shurmer (5.11)
Printed by Pureprint Group for National Trust (Enterprises) Ltd, Heelis, Kemble Drive, Swindon, Wilts SN2 2NA on Cocoon Silk made from 100% recycled paper

(*Front cover*) The castellated towers of Sizergh Castle
(*Title-page*) A huge early Victorian Staffordshire punch pot in the Entrance Hall
(*Back cover*) The oak-ribbed ceiling of the Queen's Room is based on a design by the Italian architect Sebastiano Serlio

Bibliography

Manuscript sources
The Strickland family possesses an extensive archive of deeds and family papers dating back to the 12th century. Abstracts of about 550 of these documents were prepared and arranged into a single manuscript volume by the Rev. Thomas West (*c*.1720–79), antiquary and chaplain to the Strickland family at Sizergh.

Printed sources
ANON., 'Sizergh Hall', *The Lonsdale Magazine*, iii, 30 April 1822, pp. 121–9; ANON., 'Sizergh Castle', *Country Life*, 30 June 1906, pp. 942–50; BELLASIS, Edward, 'Strickland of Sizergh', *Transactions of the Cumberland and Westmorland Antiquarian and Archaeological Society*, Old Series, x, 1889, pp. 75–94; BOURNE, Susan, and STUART, Susan, 'Sixteenth-century Furniture in the Castle Dairy, Kendal', *Regional Furniture*, v, 1991, pp. 51–9; CANNADINE, David, *Aspects of Aristocracy*, Yale University Press, 1994; CORP, Edward, and SANSON, Jacqueline, ed., *La Cour des Stuarts à Saint-Germain-en-Laye aux temps de Louis XIV*, Réunion des Musées Nationaux, Paris, 1992; CRUIKSHANKS, Eveline, and CORP, Edward, ed., *The Stuart Court in Exile and the Jacobites*, Hambledon Press, London and Rio Grande, 1995; CURWEN, John F., 'Sizergh No. 2', *TCWAAS*, Old Series, x, 1889, pp. 66–74; FARRER, William, 'Records Relating to the Barony of Kendale', i, *CWAAS Record Series*, iv, 1923; GOODALL, Ian, *Sizergh Castle*, Architectural Survey Report, National Buildings Record Index No. 99114, English Heritage, 2000; GÜRTLER, Gernot O., *TCWAAS*, lxxxix (1989), pp. 207–31; xc (1990), pp. 217–34; xciv (1994), pp. 143–69 [on Thomas Strickland, Bishop of Namur]; HALL, Samuel Carter, *The Baronial Halls and Ancient Picturesque Edifices of England*, London, 1848; HORNYOLD, Henry, *Strickland of Sizergh*, Kendal, 1928; MUSSON, Jeremy, 'Back Home to its Castle', *Country Life*, 22 June 2000, pp. 154–7; NEALE, John Preston, *Views of the Seats of Noblemen and Gentlemen in England, Wales, Scotland and Ireland*, Second Series, i, London, 1824; SCOTT, Daniel, *The Stricklands of Sizergh Castle*, Kendal, 1908; SMITH, H. Clifford, *The Panelled Rooms*, iv, *The Inlaid Room from Sizergh Castle*, Victoria and Albert Museum/HMSO, rev. edn, 1928; TAYLOR, M. W., 'Sizergh No. 1', *TCWAAS*, Old Series, x, 1889, pp. 48–65; WASHINGTON, S. H. L., 'The Early History of the Stricklands of Sizergh', *TCWAAS*, New Series, xlii, 1942, pp. 188–231, and xliv, 1944, pp. 16–54; WELLS-COLE, Anthony, *Art and Decoration in Elizabethan and Jacobean England*, Yale University Press, 1997; WENHAM, L.P., *Roger Strickland, A Jacobite Gentleman, 1680–1749*, Northallerton, 1982; WHITAKER, T.D., *An History of Richmondshire*, ii, London, 1823.

CONTENTS

A FAMILY HOME FOR SEVEN CENTURIES

Sizergh has been associated with the Strickland family since 1239, when the heiress Elizabeth Deincourt married Sir William de Stirkeland. The most imposing part of the building to survive from the medieval period is the massive tower which the Stricklands built in the mid-14th century to contain the family apartment or solar, positioned at one end of a great hall, which had a service block at its other end. The tower was a potent symbol of the Stricklands' power during the Middle Ages, when they played a leading role in the wars with Scotland and France. At the battle of Agincourt in 1415, Sir Thomas Strykeland carried the banner of St George.

The mid-1550s saw the start of a major rebuilding campaign, which was to transform the medieval house into a fashionable Elizabethan residence. This was the work of Walter Strickland (1516–69), who raised the hall to the first floor, rebuilt the medieval service block to provide more accommodation, and added two wings, one for the servants' quarters and the other for a long gallery.

Between 1558 and about 1585, the interior was fitted out with some of the finest carved and inlaid decoration ever to be seen in the north of England. The remarkable series of oak-panelled rooms culminates in the magnificent Inlaid Chamber, commissioned by Walter Strickland's widow, Alice, in the 1570s and recently returned to the house.

Prominent as Catholic royalists throughout the 17th century, the Stricklands went into exile in 1688 with the court of James II at Saint-Germain in France. They returned to Sizergh by the early 18th century as impoverished Jacobites, but thanks to the careful efforts of Winifred, Lady Strickland, they were able to afford a few baroque-style alterations to the house. The need for more drastic repairs to the first-floor hall in the 1770s, during the widowhood of Cecilia Strickland, brought about the replacement of the Elizabethan hall by a Neo-classical saloon, which later became the Drawing Room.

The last major alterations at Sizergh took place

in 1897–1902, when, among much modernisation, a neo-Gothic carriage entrance and internal staircase replaced an 18th-century external stairway to the front door. The owner at that time was Sir Gerald Strickland, later Lord Strickland of Sizergh (1861–1940), for whose second wife, Margaret Hulton, the famous rock garden was laid out in 1926–8.

In 1931 the estate was transferred to Lord Strickland's daughter Mary and her husband Henry Hornyold. They and their son Lt-Cdr Thomas Hornyold-Strickland gave the house to the National Trust in 1950, with most of the contents, the garden and an estate of 600ha (1,500 acres). Mrs Thomas Hornyold-Strickland still lives at Sizergh.

(Left) Sizergh from the south-east in 1805; by P. Atkinson (Inlaid Chamber)

Joseph Nash's 1849 lithograph of Sizergh's most famous interior, the Elizabethan Inlaid Chamber, the panelling from which was sold to the Victoria & Albert Museum in 1891 and returned to the house in 1999

Look out for the Elizabethan carved chimney-pieces. This example, dated 1564, is in the Dining Room

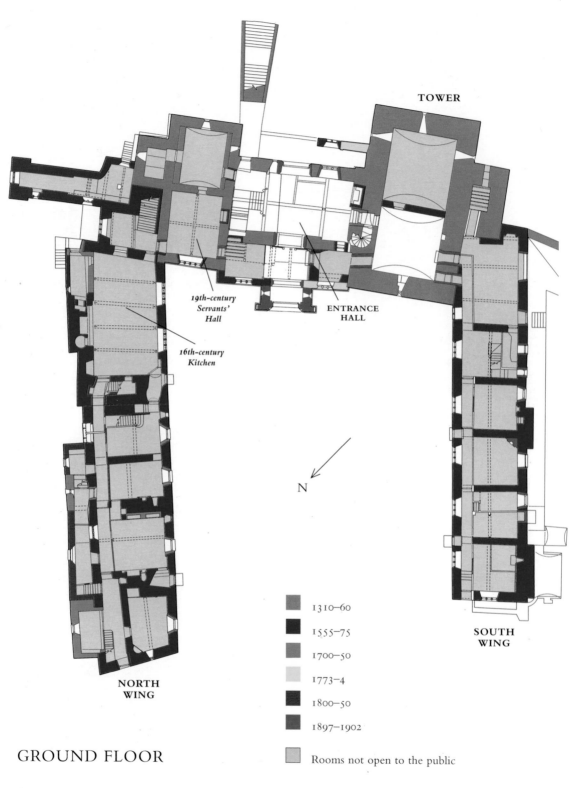

TOWER

19th-century
Servants'
Hall

ENTRANCE
HALL

16th-century
Kitchen

N

NORTH
WING

SOUTH
WING

1310–60

1555–75

1700–50

1773–4

1800–50

1897–1902

Rooms not open to the public

GROUND FLOOR

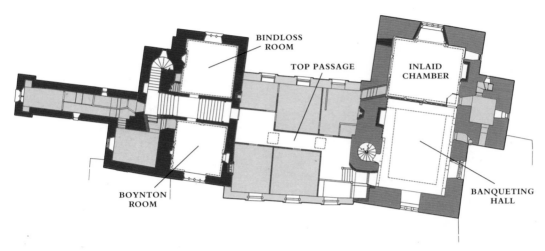

BINDLOSS ROOM

TOP PASSAGE

INLAID CHAMBER

BOYNTON ROOM

BANQUETING HALL

SECOND FLOOR

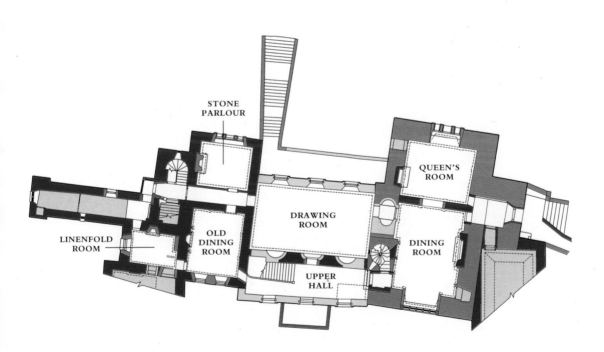

STONE PARLOUR

QUEEN'S ROOM

DRAWING ROOM

LINENFOLD ROOM

OLD DINING ROOM

DINING ROOM

UPPER HALL

FIRST FLOOR

TOUR OF THE HOUSE

THE APPROACH

Every period of Sizergh's complicated building history can be seen from the U-shaped entrance court, which forms the approach to the house. The whole of the central range between the two wings is medieval in origin, the least altered part being the four-storey tower of the mid-14th century. Battlemented and turreted, this was built to contain the solar, or principal family apartment, and proudly carries the 14th-century coat of arms of Deincourt and Strickland set in a pinnacled recess.

The central block to the left of the tower is a mid-16th-century enlargement of the medieval hall range. It was rebuilt in 1773–4 by the local architect John Hird, who installed the Gothic sash-windows and the battlemented roof, which replaced three 16th-century gables. It was altered once more in 1897–8, when the present ground-floor entrance superseded Hird's twin flights of steps to a first-floor front door. The Gothic porch, by the Kendal architect J. F. Curwen, was designed as a carriage entrance, flanked by the coats of arms of Sir Gerald Strickland (1861–1940) and his wife, Lady Edeline Sackville.

The gabled section to the left of the central block was built in about 1555, heightening the medieval service block on this site to provide additional apartments. The only later change was the insertion of a pair of early Georgian sash-windows in place of a mullioned Elizabethan

A mid-18th-century drawing of the west front, showing the 16th-century gabled central block before it was remodelled in 1773–4

The west front today

window on the first floor. The gable here has one of the most elaborate of the six pairs of Elizabethan carved oak bargeboards still surviving at Sizergh.

Other bargeboards can be seen at the ends of the flanking north and south wings, the latter built in 1558. The upper floor of the south wing was designed as an extension of the principal apartments of the tower and was originally a single room, a long gallery, over a series of self-contained lodgings – hence the ordered spacing of the windows and doors. The north wing was constructed in two stages, with an enormous kitchen built next to the central range in 1558, and other domestic offices and servants' rooms added as an extension in 1562. Both wings have seen many alterations internally in succeeding centuries, and this is reflected particularly in the north wing's patchwork of Elizabethan and Georgian window styles.

THE ENTRANCE HALL

Massive oak doors open on to a carriageway which was driven through the centre of the house in 1897–8 so that the family and guests could alight from their carriages inside the building and ascend a staircase to the upper floors. Today, however, the first feature you encounter is an impressive oak screen across the carriageway. This was brought here from the former servants' hall in 1946, but its boldly carved cresting is believed to have come originally from the Elizabethan great hall (now the Drawing Room) on the first floor. The date 1558 is inlaid on a central coffer guarded by dragons above a triangular pediment enclosing the arms of Walter Strickland (1516–69). The panelling below is 17th-century and later, but incorporates carved mid-16th-century scrolls forming an arch.

Beyond the screen, the Entrance Hall occupies the position of the lofty medieval great hall, which in the mid-1550s became a lower hall beneath a new first-floor hall. The medieval entrances in the

9

front and back walls were at the left-hand end, where the back door and a single-light window above it still survive; but the medieval access to the domestic offices at this end has been blocked by the 1890s staircase. At the opposite end, an early 18th-century round-headed doorway beside the mid-16th-century fireplace leads to the tower, but in medieval times the only access to the tower was via a staircase off the back of the hall, near the present three-light window of the 1890s.

FURNITURE

Old oak furniture dominates the Entrance Hall. The oldest piece is an early Elizabethan table with fluted legs on trestles, its later top possibly replacing one made for draw-leaves. The two oak chests, made entirely of planks dowelled together,

both have the date 1571 and the initials of Walter and Alice Strickland inlaid into a cartouche around the lock plate. Later pieces include an oak-panelled cupboard of about 1700 and a set of carved oak hall-chairs in the exuberant high-backed style of the 1690s, but probably made about two centuries later.

ARMS AND ARMOUR

Weapons were stored in medieval entrance halls to be ready in times of trouble. A collection of mostly English armour of the 16th and 17th centuries hangs from the pillars. A set of six 19th-century ceremonial spears or partisans is mounted on either side of the screen, below a pair of High Sheriff's trumpeters' banners emblazoned with the quartered arms of Strickland and Hornyold. The banners were made in 1937 for Henry Hornyold-Strickland as High Sheriff of Westmorland and were used again in 1973 by his son Thomas, who was the last High Sheriff before the old county became part of Cumbria. The foreign weapons and artefacts around the walls are of Indian, Maori or Australian origin, complementing a collection of Australian birds and mammals in display cases. These were collected by Sir Gerald Strickland during his service as a colonial governor in Australia between 1904 and 1917.

CERAMICS AND SCULPTURE

The marble bust on the window-sill is of Thomas Strickland (1792–1835) in Roman dress. It is flanked by a handsome pair of 19th-century blue-and-white Dutch Delft jugs decorated with rustic scenes from prints after François Boucher

(1703–70), bearing the monogram of Adriaenus Koeks of the Greek A factory. On a smaller window-sill is a huge early Victorian Staffordshire punch pot, unequivocally labelled 'SIZERGH RUM PUNCH'. The pair of Chinese fish bowls is of about 1800, painted in the Ming style of about three centuries earlier.

The oak staircase of 1897–8 rises to the Upper Hall.

THE UPPER HALL

The high walls of the Upper Hall were formerly hung with tapestries and now provide a gallery for family portraits and two dramatic scenes by Francis Hayman (1708–76), which originally decorated supper boxes at the Vauxhall pleasure gardens in London. *For more details of the paintings, see the*

The Entrance Hall

separate *picture list*. At the far end, formerly in the window bay of the Great Hall, an imposing mid-16th-century carved stone doorcase marks the entrance to the family apartments in the tower.

In the 16th century this room was divided into three by a pair of projecting bays, which formed part of the great hall; the divisions are still visible in the floorboards. In the early 18th century the front door to the house was placed in the recess between the bays. It was reached by an external staircase, rebuilt in 1773–4 as a double flight. The external stairs were removed in 1897–8 and the door finally became a window in the 20th century.

FURNITURE AND FURNISHINGS

The most exquisite piece here is the side-table on the half-landing. It has a top of painted plaster or scagliola, made in 1708 for Winifred Trentham, Lady Strickland (1645–1725), widow of Sir Thomas Strickland. Her monogram and the arms

(Left) The Upper Hall

The scagliola table-top on the Upper Hall stairs was made in 1708 for Winifred Trentham, Lady Strickland, and bears the Strickland and Trentham coats of arms

The Dining Room

of Strickland and Trentham can be seen in the centre.

A massive oak plank chest with inscribed and ornamented lock stands opposite the windows; this is contemporary with the two 1571 chests downstairs made for Walter and Alice Strickland. A pair of huge 19th-century Japanese Imari vases stands at either end of the chest, flanked by Chippendale-style mahogany chairs with ribanded backs, made by Gillows of Lancaster in 1765. The large ebonised bracket clock of about 1875, which performs Westminster chimes, is by Howell & James. Above is Lord Strickland's banner as Knight Grand Cross of the Order of St Michael and St George. In his lifetime it hung in St Paul's Cathedral.

THE DINING ROOM

This is on the first floor of the tower, which was built in the mid-14th century, when the whole floor would have been one large room called the solar, the family's main living apartment and at that time the only heated room in the tower. Divided into two rooms by Walter Strickland in the 1560s, this part became his great chamber, with a smaller bedchamber beyond (now the Queen's Room). Elizabethan great chambers were often the grandest of the state rooms, having taken over from the great hall as the room in which the family entertained their guests with formal dining, music, dancing and games. The room became a drawing room in the mid-18th century, but reverted to the function of a dining room in the 1890s.

CEILING AND PANELLING

The oak-panelled interior is almost entirely Elizabethan, apart from the stone-mullioned window, which was installed in 1897–8 to reinstate something approaching the format of the 16th-century one supplanted by a pair of early Georgian sash-windows. The net-like ceiling probably derives from a design published by the Italian architect Sebastiano Serlio (1475–1554).

Around the room, crisply carved, fluted columns with Corinthian capitals divide the panelling into attractive blocks of panels with an applied inner moulding which gives a coffered effect.

OVERMANTEL

The most impressive feature is the exuberantly carved overmantel in Italian Renaissance style, dated 1564. It is supported by male figures, who – appropriately for a dining room – carry baskets of fruit on their heads, while some equally festive female figures divide it into three compartments containing coats of arms nestling among scrolled foliage and figures. The central shield has four quarters denoting Strickland, Deincourt, Neville and Ward, with supporters of a stag for Ward and a bull for Neville. The coat of arms to the left has the quartered Strickland and Deincourt arms impaling (ie alongside) the quartered arms of Neville and Ward, while that to the right has Strickland, Deincourt, Neville and Ward impaling Tempest and Umfraville. Walter Strickland thus commemorated on the left his father's marriage to Katherine Neville, and on the right his own marriage to Alice Tempest.

PICTURES AND SCULPTURE

Dining rooms are traditionally hung with family portraits, and this one is distinguished by portraits of the Royal House of Stuart, painted in France during the Stricklands' exile with the Stuart court at Saint-Germain (see p. 47). The carved giltwood frames are early 18th-century French and are of exceptional quality, featuring emblems associated with the sitter in each portrait. They may have been hung in this room since the 18th century. The gilt plaster bust is of Prince Charles Edward Stuart

(1720–88), 'Bonnie Prince Charlie', copied from the 1746 original by Jean-Baptiste Lemoyne (1704–78), which is now lost.

FURNITURE

The oak extending dining-table is late 19th-century, as are most of the chairs, although their style is based on the remaining chairs, which are of about 1750, all having vase splats and red leather seats. The side-table is a Jacobean long table, which has been reduced from six legs to four; it would originally have been nearly twice its present length, matching the long table to be seen in the Banqueting Hall. Next to it is an oak cupboard of largely 17th-century origin, but reconstructed at a later date, incorporating parts of a table.

The longcase clock was made in about 1780 by Morris Thomas (active 1769–94) of Caernarfon, although the carving on its oak case is a local Victorian embellishment. The pair of fire-screens

Princess Louise-Marie, the daughter of James II, whom the Stricklands followed into exile in France in 1688; by Alexis-Simon Belle (Dining Room)

The Queen's Room

was embroidered in 1900–1 by Lady Edeline Strickland (née Sackville) with the Sackville and Strickland arms. The Strickland motto *Sans Mal* ('Without Evil') appears below the coat of arms, which is encircled by the motto of the Order of St Michael and St George, *Auspicium Melioris Aevi* ('A Sign of a Better Life').

You pass through a lobby in the 14th-century turret, which in the 16th century was the only access from the Dining Room to the Queen's Room, and to a long gallery in the south wing.

THE QUEEN'S ROOM

This 16th-century chamber would have been a place of retreat, the more exclusive in that there was no connecting door between it and the Dining Room until the mid-18th century. It would probably always have been a bedchamber, its oak-panelled walls hung with tapestries, and continued as such until the late 19th century, when it became a sitting room or small drawing room.

The room takes its name from Queen Elizabeth's coat of arms, carved in 1569 as the centrepiece of the overmantel, no doubt as a demonstration of loyalty to the Crown at a politically difficult time for Catholic families such as the Stricklands. The royal coat of arms with lion and dragon supporters is set against a ground of Tudor roses and a scroll dated 1569 proclaiming *Vivat Regina* ('Long Live the Queen').

The design of the oak ribwork ceiling is taken directly from Serlio's pattern-book, although the remarkable series of carved oak bosses in the octagons is a highly inventive local addition. The Venetian window was inserted about 1740 and may also have been based on a Serlio design.

PICTURES

Among the early family portraits are two signed in 1651 by the mysterious 'JH' – possibly Dom Jerome Hesketh, who worked as a travelling portrait painter as a cover for his then illegal activities as a Catholic priest.

FURNITURE

Loose-covered Victorian seat furniture abounds in the centre of the room but the more ornamental furniture around the walls is a mixture of mostly 18th-century English and French pieces. To the right of the window an early 18th-century walnut cushion mirror overlooks a tall Queen Anne secretaire. To the right, 1760s Chippendale-style mahogany chairs flank a French *bonheur-du-jour*, or lady's writing-table, of about 1770, made from kingwood inlaid with satinwood and ebony. The French rosewood display cabinet of similar date contains figurines and glassware.

The large marquetry cabinet to the right of the fireplace is a French Empire *secrétaire à abattant*, or upright secretaire, of kingwood inlaid with trophies of musical instruments in satinwood. To the right, a French clock in an ormolu (gilt brass) and walnut lyre-shaped case stands on a Louis XVI kingwood commode with exquisite floral inlay. The two circular tables nearby are both French, one topped with polychrome scagliola. The carpet in this room was made in the late 19th century in the Arak region of central Persia.

THE DRAWING ROOM

This room was created about 1555, when an upper floor was inserted over the medieval hall to form an Elizabethan great hall, where visitors were received and the household servants took their meals. A vast fireplace with a moulded stone arch occupied the position of the present centre window, and on the opposite side were the two bays, which projected out to the entrance front. In the early 18th century, the great hall was made into a formal entrance hall by Walter Strickland (1675–1715), who introduced a central entrance doorway reached by an external staircase.

The room took its present form in 1773–4, when the old fireplace was removed and replaced by a glazed door to the garden with large, pointed-arched windows either side. At the same time, the Upper Hall next door was created by linking the two projecting bays and inserting an internal wall which incorporated flues for heating stoves. This symmetrical arrangement of doors, windows and stoves was emphasised by setting them all into round-headed alcoves. The intention was to create a Neo-classical central hall or saloon, with doorways at either end giving access to the rest of the house. The architect was John Hird of Cartmel, commissioned by Cecilia Strickland (1741–1814), widow of Charles Strickland.

Hird's Neo-classical detailing of the interior was never completed, however, and by the 1790s the room was hung with tapestries to conceal the half-plastered walls. By 1822 it was used as a billiard room, and in the early 20th century it finally came to be called the Drawing Room, hung with family portraits. The round-headed window alcoves were later removed, when Tudor Gothic windows were inserted to match those on the floor above. However, the gold silk damask curtains and blue damask-pattern wallpaper put up in 1998 have given the room back something of its 18th-century character.

PICTURES

The family portraits include, over the door to the Upper Hall and right of the right-hand alcove, Sir Thomas and Winifred, Lady Strickland, who, as

The Drawing Room

loyal Catholics, went into exile with the deposed James II in 1688, but managed to preserve Sizergh and its estates for their eldest son, Walter (the oval portrait over the right-hand alcove).

FURNITURE

The set of eight mahogany chairs and a settee *en suite* were supplied by Gillows of Lancaster in June 1761. The settee has recently been restored and reupholstered in a red damask that has also provided loose covers for the chairs.

A notable feature of this room is its collection of English and Italian ebonised furniture inlaid with ivory in a 17th-century Italian idiom. Nineteenth-century pieces comprise *(down the centre of the room from the Dining Room end)*: an English break-front sideboard with central showcase; an Italian side-table inset with an ivory plaque representing an allegorical figure of Architecture; an Italian centre-

A rare white Mennecy soft-paste porcelain group, c.1750 (Drawing Room)

table with ebony and ivory parquetry in rosewood; an English writing-table, back-to-back with a drop-leaf occasional table carrying an Italian miniature table-cabinet; and (at the end of the room) an Italian cabinet-on-stand. Last but not least, to the left of the centre doorway, is a 17th-century Italian chest-of-drawers.

The writing-table, or *bureau Mazarin,* to the right of the centre doorway is 19th-century French. Its inlay of brass and tortoiseshell cele-brates the 1680s style of the influential French designer Jean Bérain. A French 18th-century kingwood china cabinet stands in the left-hand corner of the window wall, and in the right-hand corner is a Dutch 18th-century walnut-veneered cabinet-on-stand.

The handsome brass chandelier of 24 branches in a florid baroque style is 19th-century French.

CERAMICS

Standing tall at the Dining Room end of the room is a pair of Chinese mid-19th-century blue-ground vases made into candelabra with extremely ornate French ormolu mounts in the form of bunches of flowers. In between, the sideboard display case contains 19th-century German and English poly-chrome porcelain and is surmounted by a French 1870s clock and candelabra by Julien Le Roy in ormolu with porcelain mounts. The Italian side-table carries a pair of 19th-century Chinese celadon green vases with applied ceramic lizards and European ormolu mounts.

A collection of Nailsea glass occupies the upper shelves of the left-hand alcove, while those of the right-hand one have a collection of Georgian ceramics including Chelsea, Worcester and Derby. The centrepieces of the lower shelves are two large 20th-century porcelain vases from the Royal Copenhagen factory.

The pair of large Chinese polychrome fish bowls is of the Ch'ien Lung period, mid-18th-century. More Chinese and European porcelain of the 18th and 19th centuries can be seen in the tall china cabinet, including a rare white Mennecy soft-paste group of about 1750.

The Stone Parlour

THE STONE PARLOUR

This plain-panelled room was that referred to in 1569 as 'the chamber where Mr. Tempest lyes', the bedchamber apparently occupied by Walter Strickland's brother-in-law. It was completely refitted in the 1740s by Thomas Peter Strickland (1701–54), who installed the Venetian window, the chequered black and white stone floor which gives the room its name, and the ceiling, which has elements of Sizergh's Italian Renaissance tradition but with a hint of the newer and lighter Neoclassical manner. This ceiling may be an early work by Joseph Rose senior (*c.*1723–80), the Yorkshire plasterer famous for his work for Robert Adam

(1728–92). The room has a pleasant south-easterly aspect and has been variously used since the 18th century as a breakfast room, sitting room and study.

The columned chimneypiece (described in 1822 as 'a fire place of rich Westmorland Marble, procured upon Mr. Strickland's estate') was probably supplied by Francis Webster of Kendal about 1810 for Thomas Strickland Standish (1763–1813), using limestone from an outcrop quarry which formerly existed about a mile away near Hawes Bridge, on the River Kent. The panelling dates from the same period.

PICTURES

Over the fireplace is a portrait of Thomas Strickland (1792–1835) out hunting, painted in

1819 by the leading sporting artist, John Ferneley. Five years after this picture was completed, Thomas married into a French aristocratic family, and spent the rest of his short life in France. The other portraits are of members of the Matthews and Hoskyns families, ancestors of Henry Hornyold, who married into the Strickland family in 1920.

FURNITURE AND CERAMICS

The room is furnished mostly with Victorian and Edwardian mahogany pieces, with the notable exception of two 1840s neo-Gothic x-frame chairs, which are oak. The white marble *Head of the Young Bacchus*, mounted above the bureau in one corner, is an unsigned 19th-century work which may be Italian. The mantel clock and its garniture of candelabra in white marble and ormolu is of about 1870 by Le Roy of Paris.

THE OLD DINING ROOM

Dated 1563, this is the earliest of the Elizabethan panelled rooms and was described in 1569 as 'the chamber next Mr. Tempest chamber where thei dyne'. As such, it would have been used by family and guests for informal meals, with seating for at least twenty people on forms, stools and two panel-back armchairs for the master and mistress. Known in the 18th century as the Front Parlour, the room continued in use as the family dining room until the 1890s, when it became a morning room, an informal sitting room for the ladies. One of the few changes to the room was the insertion of a pair of early Georgian sash-windows.

OVERMANTEL, PANELLING AND CEILING

The intricately carved overmantel is emblazoned with the quartered arms of Strickland, Deincourt, Neville and Ward, shown four times on the same shield, supported by a stag for Ward and a bull for Neville. Corinthian columns divide this central compartment from the vigorous side panels of mermaid-like figures and cornucopias, and support a triangular pediment in which the bust of a classical poet appears between cartouches inlaid with the initials of Walter Strickland and the

date 1563. The high-quality panelling has lozenge-shaped inner mouldings which are echoed on the timber-ribbed ceiling.

PICTURES

Opposite the fireplace are portraits of Henry Hornyold and his wife, Mary Strickland, to whom Sizergh was transferred in 1931. They and their son Thomas gave the house, its contents and the estate to the National Trust in 1950.

FURNITURE

Among several outstanding pieces of marquetry furniture, the most notable are two Louis XVI kingwood marquetry secretaires opposite the fireplace, on either side of a late 18th-century Italian walnut and inlaid commode attributed to the Milanese cabinetmaker Giuseppe Maggiolini. Two smaller French marquetry pieces from the late 18th century stand either side of the fireplace, and opposite the windows is another, a writing-table with tambour-shuttered doors. The inlaid rosewood writing-table between the windows is Edwardian, in a style of about 1800. Above this is a mirror of about 1750, which has hung here since at least 1770. The pair to it is now to be seen in the Boynton Room above.

The earlier of the two clocks in this room is the longcase by Isaac Cockerham of Downham, Lancashire; it dates from about 1745, although the carving to the oak case is 19th-century. The other is French, a late 19th-century mantel clock mounted in ormolu on white marble columns.

THE LINENFOLD ROOM

The oak linenfold panelling dates from the early 16th century, but was reused here, probably in Elizabethan times, for what may have been a closet or small bedchamber with access to a garderobe (lavatory) in the wing beyond. Following alterations to the fireplace and window in the first half of the 18th century, the room was used as a bedroom (called the Green Room after the colour of the bed-hangings), but by the 1820s it had become a library, in which the panelling had been whitewashed. It was a smoking room in the

The Old Dining Room

The early 16th-century oak panelling in the Linenfold Room was reused from elsewhere to adorn this mid-16th-century room

later 19th century, but by 1904, when the white-wash had been stripped, it was set aside as the 'Lady Visitors' Sitting Room'.

PICTURES

The intriguing image of a gentleman scholar in his library, over the fireplace, is of the Rev. William Strickland (1731–1819) by Romney.

FURNITURE

The room is furnished mostly in old oak: William and Mary high-back chairs on either side of the fireplace; an early 17th-century writing-box on stand, and an 18th-century chest-of-drawers opposite the window. The pair of Queen Anne-style mahogany chairs with cabriole legs may have been made as a late flowering of this style in about 1740. An oak chest-of-drawers of similar date stands between them.

THE BOYNTON ROOM

This is the 16th-century bedchamber over the Old Dining Room and has panelling with a similar lozenge pattern. It has also retained its 16th-century mullioned window.

The room is named after its overmantel of 1575 incorporating the coat of arms of Sir Thomas Boynton of Barmston in Yorkshire, third husband of Alice Tempest, who lived on at Sizergh after the death of her second husband, Walter Strickland, in 1569. The arms of Boynton impaling Tempest are surmounted by a horned grotesque, signifying the Boynton crest of a goat, within a tight composition of scrolled foliage and mythical beasts. The Regency chimneypiece dates from about 1810, and like that in the Stone Parlour it is of local polished limestone carved at Webster's marble yard in Kendal. It has been fitted with an Arts and Crafts fire grate of about 1900.

FURNITURE

The 16th-century oak tester bed with turned foot-posts was once decoratively panelled with inlaid floral roundels in the ceiling of the tester, and applied arabesques in the headboard. The Venetian point lace bedspread was made in 1919 by Belgian war-refugees for Lady Inglefield of Ambleside.

The pier-glass in a white and giltwood frame is of a pair with that in the Old Dining Room and has retained its original 1750s glass plate.

THE BINDLOSS ROOM

This is the room over the Stone Parlour and has similarly plain, but 17th-century panelling, reset and added to in the 1850s to accommodate the carved oak overmantel from which the room takes its name. The overmantel came from Borwick Hall, near Carnforth, an Elizabethan house built by a Kendal cloth merchant, Robert Bindloss (d. 1595). Borwick was inherited by Thomas Strickland in 1807, remaining in the Strickland family until sold in 1854. Dated 1629, the coat of arms commemorates Sir Francis Bindloss (d. 1628) and his wife, Cecilia West, daughter of the Lord De La Warr who, as Governor of Virginia, perpetuated his name in the state and river of Delaware.

The brown speckled marble chimneypiece installed in the 1850s at the same time as the overmantel. It carries an 1880s clock by E. Gleizes fils of Paris, in the form of a drum surmounted by Cupid and borne by an elephant.

PICTURES

Left of the door is a portrait of Lady Edeline Sackville, who married the future Lord Strickland in 1890. They visited Sizergh as often as his career in Maltese politics and as a colonial governor would allow. The other portraits are of Lady Edeline's Sackville relations.

FURNITURE

The oak half-tester bed was made up from fragments of the 16th-century Strickland family pew, discarded during restoration work at Kendal parish church in the 1850s. The carving of the lion masks

The oak bed in the Bindloss Room was put together in the mid-19th century, using some pieces of genuine 16th-century carved woodwork

and grotesques on the headboard relates to similar Elizabethan work at Sizergh and includes what may be a 'Boynton goat' mask of the 1570s. The 16th-century work is complemented by some 1850s armorial carving on the footboard showing the holly crest and the three scallop shells of the Strickland coat of arms, together with the Strickland motto, the date 1858 and the initials of Walter Charles Strickland.

The pair of mahogany tallboys with Chinese-style fretwork frieze was made by Gillows of Lancaster for Walter and Margaret Strickland in 1758.

THE TOP PASSAGE

Rising above the Drawing Room and Upper Hall, the Top Passage serves a series of largely featureless bedrooms, which were part of the rebuilding of 1773–4, but not fitted out until the early 19th century. The way through to the second floor of the tower was made later, but before 1852.

The overmantel in the Boynton Room was carved in 1575 for Sir Thomas Boynton, who, with his wife, Alice Strickland, also created the Inlaid Chamber

FURNITURE AND FURNISHINGS

Nineteenth-century French-style cabinetmaking is in evidence here. On the first landing, a delicate rosewood inlaid cabinet of drawers stands in company with a tall mahogany china cabinet displaying 18th-century German figurines; and at the end of the passage, past a 17th-century Flemish verdure tapestry, a 1740-style black and gilt 'tabernacle' mirror of c.1900 hangs beside an elaborate Boulle cabinet inlaid with brass and tortoiseshell and carrying a Canton vase, opposite a French walnut and ebonised display cabinet of Chinese porcelain.

The large white marble figure of a woman surprised while bathing was carved by E. Bertuzzi of Rome in 1875.

THE BANQUETING HALL

In medieval times, the second floor of the tower was the solar chamber, the family's main sleeping apartment. The western half, now known as the Banqueting Hall, is lit by a 14th-century three-light window overlooking the courtyard and has a mid-16th-century fireplace and adze-hewn oak boards on massive diagonally laid joists. The spiral staircase provided the only access until the 19th century, when a doorway was cut through from the Top Passage. This was probably part of the mid-19th-century alterations inspired by the fashion for romantic medievalism which created a highly theatrical interior. The removal of the floor above made a double-height hall, open to the 16th-century roof timbers. Late 19th- and early 20th-century photographs show the walls painted with *trompe-l'oeil* ashlar stonework and hung with armour and trophies of weapons in true baronial style. In 1948 Henry Hornyold-Strickland made a gallery around all four sides, using timber salvaged from a 16th-century barn which had collapsed in 1945.

FURNITURE

Among the 16th- and 17th-century oak furniture in this room are some of Sizergh's most distinguished pieces. Against the early 17th-century long-table are two sets of four Elizabethan forms, or benches, the sides carved to imitate the loosely hanging edge of a hide covering. One set has the initials of Walter Strickland and the date 1562, while the other may be slightly later and made to match. A 1569 inventory includes two sets of '4 short furmes' valued at 1s 6d each. Chairs with arms were comparatively scarce in the mid-16th century, and indeed the 1569 inventory records only nine in the whole house. The four panel-back chairs with flat-topped arms are of that period, three of them with lozenge panels matching those in the Old Dining Room and dated 1570 and 1571, the fourth with an inset rectangular moulding similar to the present Dining Room panelling. The remaining two armchairs have later, downward-scrolled arms: a panel-back of about 1600 and a slat-back of about 1700. The two chairs without arms, known in early inventories as back-stools, are mid-17th-century of south Yorkshire

The Banqueting Hall in 1934, when it was furnished in baronial style

(Left) The Banqueting Hall

type, each having the typical pair of arched back-rails but in this case with the lower rail rather oddly mounted upside-down to form a circle.

Dining chambers commonly had a press cupboard with various compartments for storing pewter and other tableware. The two-stage, heavily carved cupboard in this room is of about 1680, and on the table are displayed some of the pewter chargers of that period, stamped with the arms of Sir Thomas Strickland (1621–94). The Strickland arms can also be seen in moulded form on the set of 17th-century green glass bottles.

The tall, plain-panelled cupboard dated 1698 and the Georgian arched-panelled cupboard are both clothes presses, for storing clothes laid flat on sliding shelves. Between them are two oak linen chests, one with late 17th-century carved panels,

This panel-back armchair in the Banqueting Hall is dated 1571

the other solidly Elizabethan (albeit supporting a Bible box dated 1772) and provided with three locks, probably for keeping secure the most valuable of the textiles.

An equally secure, but more decorative, chest can be seen in the main window bay. This is a Nuremberg armoured chest dated 1623, bound with iron but also at one time delicately gilded and painted with naturalistic flowers on a green ground. Another example of German metalwork is the giant sword which hangs on the opposite side of the room. Variously known as a 'hand-and-a-half' or 'bastard' sword of 'lowland' type, it was made about 1540, but in a style of two centuries earlier. It may be the 'two handyt Sworde' which appears in a list of 'armore' at Sizergh in 1569.

TAPESTRY

The late 17th-century Brussels tapestry portrays the Roman Emperor Marcus Aurelius (AD121–80) reproving his wife Faustina for her profligate living.

THE INLAID CHAMBER

This magnificent state bedchamber is the culmination in the Elizabethan work at Sizergh. Between about 1575 and the mid-1580s it was fitted out with elaborate plasterwork and the inlaid oak panelling from which it takes its name, for Alice Strickland and her third husband, Sir Thomas Boynton. Complete with its domed and arcaded corner porch, heraldic glass, and carved and inlaid state bed, the room would always have been the showpiece of the house, reserved for honoured guests.

Unlike the other panelled rooms, it has no carved overmantel, and if one had ever been made for this room, it had disappeared by 1805, when a landscape was painted to fit above the mid-16th-century fireplace, flanked by replica pilasters made in pine and grained to match the oak ones elsewhere. This and other consciously antiquarian restorations in this room were the work of Cecilia Strickland (1741–1814); but in 1891 her great-grandson, Walter C. Strickland, fell upon hard times and decided to offer the panelling for sale. It

The Inlaid Chamber

was purchased for £1,000 by the Victoria and Albert Museum, where it was displayed beneath a plastercast of the ceiling. Five years later the museum purchased the bed and armorial stained-glass roundels for £400 to add to the display.

The loss of this panelled room was much regretted by later generations at Sizergh, and in 1973 the museum returned on loan two sections of the panelling, followed in 1978 by the bed. Finally, in 1998, the museum's plans for a major reorganisation of its British Galleries provided the opportunity for returning the whole of the panelling to Sizergh on long loan, and in 1999 it was transported back, conserved and reinstalled.

PANELLING

The inlaid panelling is among the finest ever made for an English country house. Its architectural forms and motifs are predominantly those of the Italian Renaissance, perhaps received via Flemish pattern-books. Ionic pilasters divide the room into bays with Italianate round-headed arcading in the upper panels and five-panelled framing in the lower. All the main panels and friezes are inlaid on a sumptuously large scale, with geometrical strapwork and foliated scrolls which use inlays of poplar (a light-coloured wood) and bog-oak (a shiny black wood found in peat bogs) to create a shimmering interplay of light and dark. In addition, there is evidence that a black stain was applied to some of the undecorated recesses and fluting to make a greater contrast with the inlaid panels, which are of light oak with an attractively feathered grain.

The pattern of the inlay in the arcaded upper panels is of vigorous arabesques, some having interlaced lozenges at the centre, where those on the fireplace wall have a fleur-de-lis, and those in the window a crescent derived from the Boynton coat of arms. The inlay in the central compartment of the eighteen lower panels has more than a dozen different patterns of scrollwork and inter-lacing, while the geometrical pattern of the skirting remains constant around the room. There is a similar unifying effect in the scrollwork of the upper and middle friezes.

PORCH

The three-sided corner porch, contrived for privacy as well as draught-proofing, is a most accomplished piece of architecture and may have been the last part of the room to be completed. Its predominantly Flemish design is almost certainly taken from the late 16th-century pattern-book of Hans Vredeman de Vries of Antwerp (1527–c.1604). Although not inlaid, it follows the rest of the room in having five-panelled framing in the lower part and an arcaded upper tier, above which is a domed roof surmounted by a carved figure of Cupid. The lion masks on the upper panels are a distinctive feature seen elsewhere, not only at Sizergh; others that may have been carved by the same hand are to be found in the 16th-century Castle Dairy in Kendal.

CEILING

Above the panelling is a moulded plaster frieze of two alternating patterns, the background of which has been picked out in yellow ochre distemper, probably in the late 19th century. This leads up to a superbly decorative ceiling of ribbed plasterwork with wreathed armorial plaques set among eight-pointed stars and pendants. The design of the ribbing is much like that devised for Henry VIII's Great Watching Chamber at Hampton Court Palace in the early 1530s, except that it probably copies the Serlio pattern-book in having a roundel in the centre of each of the pointed cross shapes.

Six of these roundels across the middle of the ceiling contain coats of arms, two for each of three families: Strickland quartered with Deincourt, Neville and Ward *(centre row)*; Boynton quartered with Old Boynton, Delsee and Monceaux *(row nearer the window wall)*; and Tempest quartered with Umfraville *(row nearer the wall opposite the window)*. Roundels in the rest of the ceiling contain one of two heraldic beasts: a goat, the crest of the Boynton family; and a stag, one of the supporters of the Strickland coat. Four other large-scale moulds incorporating flowers, fruits or fleurs-de-lis are each used in alternating pairs or fours to fill the remaining spaces. The ceiling of the bay has a plaster ribwork pattern of its own, in which the quartered Strickland arms occupies the centre, while the surrounding ribs are sprouting with single leaves and flowers in five different forms. The moulded decoration has retained an exceptional crispness, because the ceiling has been whitewashed only very rarely in its 400-year history.

While the identity of the plasterers is unknown,

The internal porch reduced draughts and offered greater privacy

it would appear that in the late 1580s they went on to work for Sir James Bellingham at Levens Hall, reusing many of the moulds employed at Sizergh.

STAINED GLASS

The window, arcaded to match the panelling, is an Elizabethan enlargement of a smaller medieval window, which had been supplemented by two others now obscured by the panelling, to the left of the fireplace and to the right of the bed. The window was reglazed in 1999 to incorporate the original stained-glass roundels within leaded clear glazing of Crown glass type, repeating the lozenge pattern shown in Joseph Nash's drawing of 1849. This glazing pattern is Elizabethan in style, but not in scale; it probably dates from the antiquarian restorations of about 1805, as window glass would not have been available in such large sizes in Elizabethan times.

The first three of the stained-glass roundels are 16th-century, all showing the quartered arms of Deincourt and Strickland on the left side of the shield, but with impalements on the right side denoting (i) Pennington, (ii) Roos and Parr, and (iii) Beetham and Burton. The fourth is an unrelated early 19th-century quatrefoil, which presumably replaces a lost 16th-century original.

FURNITURE

The bed is contemporary with the panelling but has been much restored, probably in the late 18th century. A 1785 inventory of this room lists 'a Venerable Old Oak Carved bed with Teaster & head board & Posts all repair'd 1779 by Abreham Story Cabenitmaker'. Story had earlier been described as house carpenter and in 1772 had been paid for 'work in repairing Old wainscote in ye inlay'd chamber'. Various repairs to the bed are attributable to him: the revamping of the head-board with its carved figures separating arcaded panels inlaid in walnut on poplar; the renewal of the panelled oak plinths supporting the magnificent pair of Italian Renaissance footposts of carved walnut; and, most interestingly, the reworking of the canopy or tester, where the frieze matches that of the panelling, except that the 'inlay' used here is linseed-oil putty. Above is the

The famous Elizabethan panelling in the Inlaid Chamber returned to Sizergh from the Victoria & Albert Museum in 1999

carved coat of arms of Walter Strickland dated 1568, an earlier date than the rest of the room. This piece of carving has evidently been reused, either from an earlier bed or from a destroyed overmantel. After the repairs of 1779, the bed was decked out in the high-quality scarlet moreen hangings which still survive. Moreen is a fine wool worsted that has been folded on itself and pressed to give the appearance of watered silk, and this is a rare and well-preserved example of that material.

Standing nearby is an English bentside spinet in a walnut case, one of the few surviving instruments by the late 17th-century harpsichord-maker John Player. It was to be found in the hall (now the Drawing Room) in 1770, when it was described as 'a small old Spinett much out of repair'.

Oak benches and backstools are the seat furniture here – that at the dressing-table being a Lancashire panel-back with the characteristic pyramid finials.

PLAN OF THE GARDEN

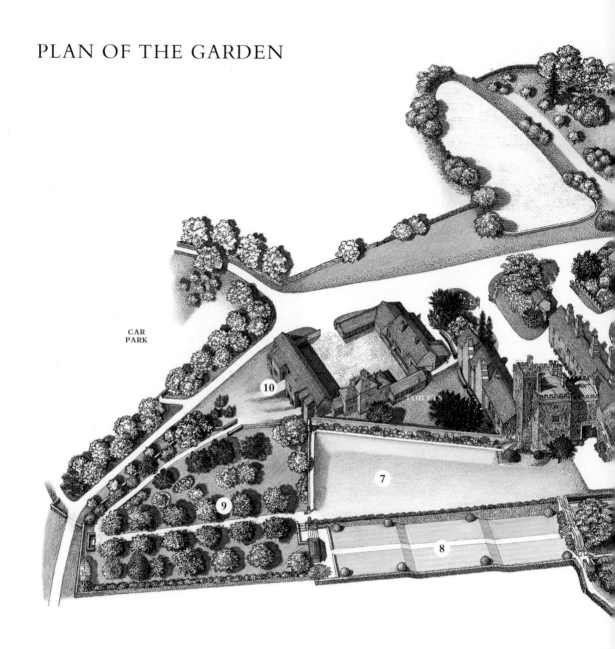

CAR
PARK

10

7

9

8

1 Small Orchard
2 Herbaceous Border
3 Rock Garden
4 Wildflower Bank
5 Lake

6 Terrace
7 Main Lawn
8 Dutch Garden
9 South Garden
10 Great Barn

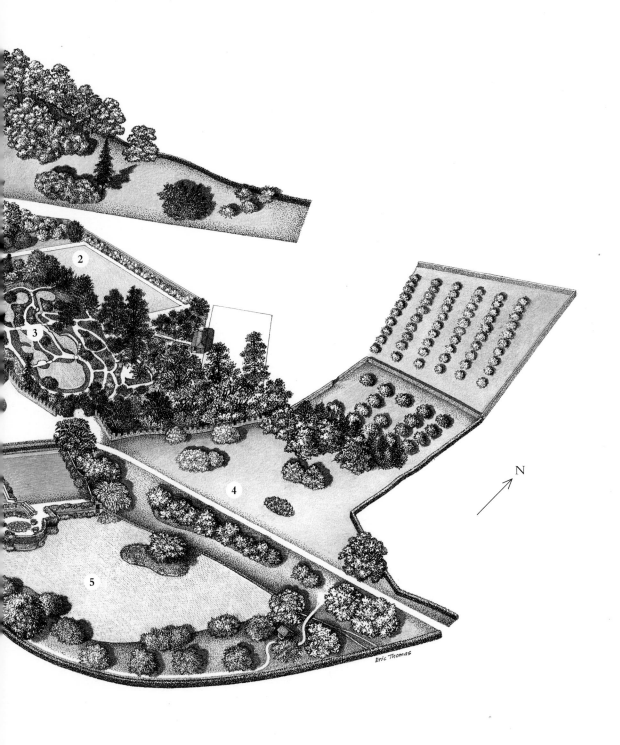

N

Eric Thomas

THE GARDEN

The oldest part of the garden is the terraced lawn that extends south-westwards from the house, bounded on one side by a brick-faced fruit wall and on the other by a stone retaining wall. This area was laid out in the mid-18th century, after the brick wall had been built in 1739, and has a vista along the wall to an elegant classical recess or summer-house. A pair of urn-surmounted gate-piers at the far end of the lawn is part of the same scheme; the gates originally opened into the deer-park, but by the mid-19th century an avenue of beeches linked the gateway to the south drive, making this a formal approach to the house. Surrounding the avenue there was an area of yew woodland, which may have been maintained as a pheasantry.

The remainder of the present garden to the east and north was created in 1926–8 from an earlier south-east-facing embankment overlooking marshy ground, and a walled area to the north, which had previously been cultivated as an orchard. A formal terrace was constructed on the embankment, with steps leading down to a small lake, while an enclosed strip to the south was made into an elaborate Dutch garden. The enclosure to the north of the house was laid out as a rock garden, with blocks of local water-worn limestone and a series of pools and rivulets flowing out of a catchment pond and draining into the lake. This work of 1926–8, believed to have been designed by a local architect, Charles Henry Wearing, was carried out by T. R. Hayes & Sons of Ambleside for Sir Gerald Strickland and his second wife, Margaret.

Since 1940, the beech avenue has been replaced, the yews pollarded, and a rose garden laid out, while to the north of the Rock Garden a new lawn and herbaceous border have been established on the site of a kitchen garden.

The development of the many diverse elements at Sizergh, within an area of 5.6ha (14 acres), has been assisted by the relatively mild and temperate nature of the climate, the presence of lime in the soil here and there, the moderately high annual rainfall (1270mm or 50in) and the generally sheltered position of the garden within the rolling landscape of south-east Cumbria.

TOUR OF THE GARDEN

From the front door of the house, the route to the garden is on the right at the upper end of the courtyard, passing the end of the North Wing and continuing down. The tour follows a generally clockwise route, finishing near the Great Barn and the car-park.

THE SMALL ORCHARD

A group of old crab-apple trees (*Malus pumila* 'Dartmouth') in the centre of the walled garden is all that remains of the orchard on this site. To the right of the gravel path and sheltered by the terrace wall are two spreading cherries (*Prunus pubescens* 'Shirotae') and the Himalayan *Hydrangea aspera* var. *macrophylla,* with large pale blue flowers. At the end of the orchard, overlooking the lawn, are two Katsura trees (*Cercidiphyllum japonicum*) noted for their splendid yellow foliage and fragrance of strawberries in autumn. Nearby is a young Caucasian Wingnut (*Pterocarya fraxinifolia*). The whole area is underplanted with spring bulbs including Snake's Head Fritillary (*Fritillaria meleagris*) and the Victorian double Wood Anemone (*Anemone* × *ranunculoïdes* 'Vestal').

The garden front and lake

THE HERBACEOUS BORDER

The lawn to the right of the path was a vegetable garden until the 1960s. The slope on the left, above the seat, is planted with Snow Pear (*Pyrus nivalis*) behind a Weeping Silver Lime, *Tilia paucicostata* 'Petiolaris'. In the top corner is *Prunus padus* 'Colorata', a pink form of Bird Cherry, contrasting with the more architectural, spine-toothed foliage of *Berberis pruinosa*.

The scheme of the long border is of soft colours running to a centre of hot colours, with contrasts in foliage types. The back wall supports a number of climbing roses, the oldest being 'Blush Noisette', the original rose developed by Philippe Noisette in the early 19th century. Along the wall are good specimens of the colourful Chinese climber *Actinidia kolomikta,* the tender Andean climbing daisy *Mutisia oligodon,* and the pale pink hybrid jasmine *Jasminum × stephanense.*

Border plants of vivid colour and interest are *Fritillaria imperialis,* the Crown Imperial, producing large orange or yellow flowers in spring; *Nepeta govaniana,* a yellow-flowered catmint from India; *Lathyrus vernus,* the Spring Pea, a large-flowered species cultivated in England as early as 1629; and *Lobelia perpusilla* 'Queen Victoria' with purple foliage bearing scarlet spikes in late summer. Tall yellow spikes of Foxtail Lily (*Eremurus bungei*), contrast with the pencil-veined flowers of *Geranium renardii* at the edge of the border.

The Rock Garden in June

A gate at the end of the Herbaceous Border leads to a kitchen garden which was opened in 2003 to produce vegetables, fruit, flowers and herbs for use in Sizergh's café. Old and modern varieties are cultivated, and there is an unusual knee-high apple hedge as a surround to the beds.

Beyond is an orchard of 50 different varieties of apple, many of them northern cultivars such as 'Keswick Codlin' and 'Carlisle Codlin', together with plum, damson and pear.

THE ROCK GARDEN

Several factors combine to make this unique among rock gardens: its large extent; its use of weathered limestone from local outcrops; its high proportion of native species rather than cultivars; and its extensive range of conifers and hardy ferns.

The collection of about 75 species of conifer includes many dwarf varieties that have grown exceptionally broad. The higher beds have numerous 'bun' forms of Norway Spruce – the Christmas Tree – such as *Picea abies* 'Ellwangeriana' and *P. a.* 'Pseudomaxwellii'; these two can be found in front of the pavilion, together with a Caucasian

Fir in its prostrate form, *Abies nordmanniana* 'Pendula'.

Various Japanese maples enhance the central area of the Rock Garden, notably *Acer palmatum atropurpureum*, with its bronzy crimson foliage, and a cut-leaved form, *A. p.* var. *dissectum atropurpureum*, overlooked by a mature *Acer palmatum* which originated from seed collected in Japan in the early 1920s. All give brilliant autumn colours. A fine specimen of the golden West Felton Yew (*Taxus baccata* 'Dovastonii Aurea') overhangs a pool by the orchard wall.

The rock garden excels in its hardy fern collection of about 175 species and cultivars. The Tatting Fern (*Athyrium filix-femina* 'Frizelliae multifidum'), is one of about 20 forms of Lady Fern to be found here. Below a large Bhutan Pine (*Pinus wallichiana*), is the cut-leaved Royal Fern (*Osmunda regalis corymbiferum*), while the centre bed of the Rock Garden contains the Japanese Painted Fern (*Athyrium nipponicum* var. *pictum*), with its grey and maroon colouring. Many Victorian hardy fern introductions survive here, and Sizergh now has the National Collection of four genera, namely the Bladder, Hartstongue, Male and Royal ferns with their many forms.

Colour throughout the season is provided by a range of woodland geraniums, aquatic plants, primulas in spring, rodgersias in July and the handsome Willow-leaved Gentian in late summer. The large yellow spathes of the American Skunk Cabbage (*Lysichiton americanus*) appear at the water's edge in spring, along with the white spathes of its Russian cousin, *L. camtschatcensis*. Both have a weird and sickly banana-like smell.

THE WILDFLOWER BANK

Native Lakeland daffodils appear on the grassy slopes in spring, followed by a wide range of local limestone flora. The Greater Butterfly Orchid and the locally scarce Fly Orchid are two of several native orchids to be found here.

THE LAKE

The beds on the right of the drive contain Sumachs (*Rhus typhina*) for autumn colour, together with *Viburnum plicatum* 'Mariesii', Purple Smoke Bush (*Cotinus coggygria rubrifolius*), newly planted *Cercis*, and a selection of species roses including Farrer's Threepenny-bit Rose, *Rosa farreri* var. *persetosa*.

Among evergreens at the far side of the lake is a group of Manna Ash (*Fraxinus ornus*) noted for foamy and fragrant white flowers in summer, and the red-stemmed willow, *Salix alba vitellina* 'Britzensis'. Around the lake, recent planting has introduced Corkscrew Hazel (*Corylus avellana* 'Contorta'), Purple Hazel (*C. maxima* 'Purpurea') and various flowering currants. A solitary and newly planted specimen of Weeping Hornbeam (*Carpinus betulus* 'Pendula') occupies the island.

Narcissi *and* Lysichiton americanus *(Yellow Skunk Cabbage) in the Rock Garden in spring*

35

The gateway to the South Garden from the Main Lawn

The lake, which was made in 1928, was dredged for the first time in 1984 and stocked with Golden Rudd. The spread of water lilies is controlled in order to maintain the superb reflection of the house from the opposite bank.

THE TERRACE

Vines and clematis cling to the 1920s parapet above the lake – with *Vitis coignetiae* showing the richest autumn colouring – and in July the tall conifers above the boathouse become conspicuous in a white mantle of Russian Vine, *Fallopia baldschuanica*.

The steps to the house, narrowing at the top to exaggerate perspective, are draped in mauve *Erinus alpinus,* the May-flowering Fairy Foxglove, and the pink and white *Erigeron karvinskianus* in summer and autumn. In the side beds are Alpine Mint Bush (*Prostanthera cuneata*), bearing tubular white flowers, *Libertia ixioides*, a perennial producing clusters of white saucer-shaped flowers, and *Spartium junceum*, a deciduous shrub with showy, pea-like flowers of golden yellow. The border below the tower has alliums and *Dierama pulcherrimum.*

THE MAIN LAWN

The southern angle of the tower shelters a group of fig 'Brown Turkey' and the bluish-green sword-leaved *Beschorneria yuccoïdes*, a mountain woodland plant from Mexico. Beyond is the long, brick-faced 'hot wall' built in 1739. The limestone core is faced with brick to retain warmth for fruit trees on cordons.

It now supports pears and vines in alternate bays. The bed below the wall is planted with an array of bulbs giving colour from spring to autumn.

The narrow border on the opposite side of the lawn contains a delicate hedge of *Fuchsia magellanica,* which is pruned down each year to allow an early show of *Scilla siberica* 'Spring Beauty', forming a ribbon of rich blue.

THE DUTCH GARDEN

Intricate flower-beds were devised for the Dutch Garden in 1926 on the site of an earlier small orchard, but only the basic terracing survived its return to rough grass in 1949.

The terraces were reclaimed from parkland in 1984 and later planted with an avenue of cherries, *Prunus* 'Tai Haku', giving a dazzling a show of white in spring and some rich autumn colour. The blue and white effect of thousands of *Scilla* and *Chionodoxa* bulbs is a further enhancement in spring. The limestone retaining wall is planted with alpines.

In front of the summer-house, pale pink *Abelia × grandiflora* adds fragrance to the border below the retaining wall. A large-flowered variety of lily of the valley from Hardwick Hall (NT) can be seen in the opposite border.

THE SOUTH GARDEN

The yew avenue, planted in 1996, and shaped into pyramids, is on the site of an avenue of beeches which became unsafe in the 1940s and had to be felled. The formal yew hedge around the stone seat is enlivened by the bright scarlet flowers of Scottish Flame Flower (*Tropaeolum speciosum*).

On either side, the South Garden has recently been simplified around specimen trees and shrubs to give a more open feel. Above the avenue are large specimens of autumn flowering *Eucryphia × nymansensis* 'Nymansay', and *Magnolia × soulangeana*, with its pink, shaded purple flowers in spring,

while at the exit gate a *Davidia involucrata* can be seen displaying its unusual handkerchief bracts in late May.

THE GREAT BARN

Reputed to have been built by Walter Strickland in the 1560s, this may be the earliest known example of a two-storey Lake District bank barn, in which animals are housed at ground level and hay and grain are stored on an upper floor accessible from a ramp or a bank. In 1569 'the new barne' contained wheat, barley and oats, together with a large number of agricultural implements. Livestock included 22 oxen and twelve horses, serving a prosperous and self-sufficient farm.

The Great Barn, conspicuously sited near the southern approach to the castle, was clearly meant to show off the status of its owner. It is impressively large, measuring over 100ft (30.5m) in length, and has the rare distinction of having not one, but two, ramps and two sets of double doors to the upper level. Another unusual feature on the south side is a series of small outshuts (projecting buildings) ranged against it. The middle one, between the ramps, is at first-floor level only, supported at the centre by a circular stone pillar. This would almost certainly have been used to store milled grain. The upper floor of the barn, with its double row of ventilation slits in the walls, has changed comparatively little since the 16th century.

The Great Barn shares the yard with several other estate buildings. The west range (now a row of garages) is the remnant of what was described in 1569 as 'the haye barne'. The east range comprises the late 18th-century coach-house and stable, attributable to the architect John Hird. It was converted to accommodation in the 1920s.

FAMILY TREE

Owners of Sizergh are in CAPITALS

Asterisk denotes a portrait on show

Places named are in Cumbria unless otherwise stated

GERVASE DEINCOURT (d. by 1211) Granted Sizergh 1175–80 by William de Lancaster Lord of Kendal

Adam de Castlecarrock (living 1179)

Sir Walter fitz Adam (alias de Strikeland) Kt c.1230 (d. by 1239) = Christian de Leteham (d. c.1238) heiress of Great Strickland

Sir Ralph Deincourt of Sizergh (d. by 1233) = Eleanor le Fleming of Furness

Sir Ralph Deincourt of Sizergh (living 1251) = Alice de Thursby (living 1260) coheiress

Robert de Castlecarrock

Robert de Stirkeland (d. c.1230) = Beatrice de Cotesford of Asby

main line died out c.1300

Adam fitz Walter no issue

Sir Robert de Stirkeland (d. c.1278) of Great Strickland = – de Genellestane (living 1271)

Sir William de Stirkeland Kt 1280 (d. c.1305) of Great Strickland and Sizergh = Elizabeth Deincourt (d. by 1276) m.1239 heiress of Sizergh and other lands in N. and S. Westmorland

Sir Walter de Stirkeland Kt 1308 (d. c.1343) of Sizergh = (1) Eleanor de Goldington m.1296, div. 1298 (2) Matilda

Sir William = Margaret (d. c.1288) of Great Strickland

Sir Thomas de Stirkeland Kt by 1335 (d. 1376) = Cecily de Welles (d.c.1387) m.1323

Sir Walter de Stirkeland Kt c.1380 (d. 1407) = (1) Margaret de Lathom m.1366 (2) Alice –

Sir Thomas Strykeland Kt by 1429 (d. 1455) = Mabel de Bethom m.1405

Walter Strickland (c.1412–c.1467) = Douce Croft m.1426

Sir Thomas Strickland Kt 1471 (d.c.1497) = (1) Agnes Parr (d.c.1490) m.1464 (2) Margaret, Lady Byron m.1491

Sir Walter Strickland KB 1501 (d. 1506) = Elizabeth Pennington (d.1546) m.1491

Sir Walter Strickland Kt 1523 (1497–1528) = Katherine Neville m.1515 inherited Thornton Bridge, Yorks., and her mother's Ward estates

Walter Strickland (1516–69) of Sizergh and Thornton Bridge = (1) Agnes Hamerton m.1536 (2) Alice Tempest (d.1588) m.1560 = (3) Sir Thomas Boynton of Barmston, Yorks. (d.1581) m.1573

Sir Thomas Strickland*, KB 1603 (1564–1612) of Sizergh and Thornton Bridge bought Sedbergh Manor 1598–1601 = (1) – Seymour of Bristol (2) Margaret Curwen

Walter = Anne Croft (d. by 1677)

Sir Robert Strickland* Kt 1641 (1600–71) of Sizergh and Thornton Bridge = Margaret Alford m.1619

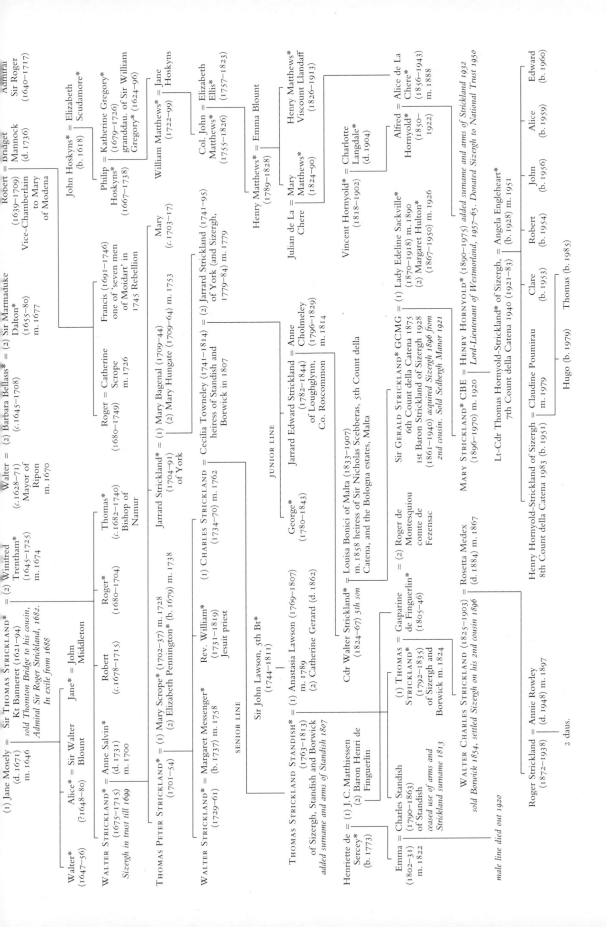

Admiral
Sir Roger
(1640–1717)

Robert = Bridget
(1639–1709) Mannock
Vice-Chamberlain (d. 1736)
to Mary
of Modena

John Hoskyns = Elizabeth
(b. 1618) Scudamore*

Philip = Katherine Gregory*
Hoskyns* (1679–1726)
(1667–1738) granddau. of Sir William
Gregory* (1624–96)

Walter = (2) Sir Marmaduke
(c. 1628–71) Dalton*
Mayor of (1655–80)
Ripon m. 1677
m. 1670

William Matthews* = Jane
(1722–99) Hoskyns

Mary
(c. 1703–17)

Francis (1691–1746)
one of 'seven men
of Moidart' in
1745 Rebellion

Roger = Catherine
(1680–1749) Scrope
m. 1726

Col. John = Elizabeth
Matthews* Ellis*
(1755–1826) (1757–1823)

Jarrard Strickland (1741–95)
of York (and Sizergh,
1779–84) m. 1779

Henry Matthews* = Emma Blount
(1789–1828)

Henry Matthews*
Viscount Llandaff
(1826–1913)

Julian de La = Mary
Chere Matthews*
(1824–90)

Jarrard Strickland* = (1) Mary Bagenal (1709–44)
(1704–91) (2) Mary Hungate (1709–64) m. 1753
of York

Vincent Hornyold* = Charlotte
(1818–1902) Langdale*
(d. 1904)

Alfred = Alice de La
Hornyold* Chere*
(1830– (1856–1943)
1922) m. 1888

(1) Charles Strickland = Cecilia Towneley (1741–1814) (2) Jarrard Strickland
(1734–70) m. 1762 heiress of Standish and
Borwick in 1807

JUNIOR LINE

Jarrard Edward Strickland = Anne
(1782–1844) Cholmeley
of Loughglynn, (1796–1829)
Co. Roscommon m. 1814

Sir Gerald Strickland* GCMG = (1) Lady Edeline Sackville*
6th Count della Catena 1875 (1870–1918) m. 1890
1st Baron Strickland of Sizergh 1928 (2) Margaret Hulton*
(1861–1940) acquired Sizergh 1896 from (1867–1950) m. 1926
2nd cousin. Sold Sedbergh Manor 1921

Edward
(b. 1960)

Alice
(b. 1959)

John
(b. 1956)

Robert
(b. 1954)

Clare
(b. 1953)

Mary Strickland* CBE = Henry Hornyold* (1890–1975) added surname and arms of Strickland 1932
(1896–1970) m. 1920 Lord-Lieutenant of Westmorland, 1957–65. Donated Sizergh to National Trust 1950

Walter*
(1647–56)

(1) Jane Mosely = Sir Thomas Strickland*
(d. 1671) Kt Banneret (1621–94)
m. 1646 sold Thornton Bridge to his cousin,
Admiral Sir Roger Strickland, 1682.
In exile from 1688

= (2) Winifred
Trentham*
(1645–1725)
m. 1674

Alice* = Sir Walter
(?1648–80) Blount

Walter Strickland* = Anne Salvin*
(1675–1715) (d. 1731)
Sizergh in trust till 1699 m. 1700

Roger*
(1680–1704)

Robert
(c. 1678–1715)

Thomas*
(c. 1682–1740)
Bishop of
Namur

Jane* = John
Middleton

Thomas Peter Strickland* = (1) Mary Scrope* (1702–37) m. 1728
(1701–54) (2) Elizabeth Pennington* (b. 1679) m. 1738

Walter Strickland* = Margaret Messenger*
(1729–61) (b. 1737) m. 1758

Rev. William*
(1731–1819)
Jesuit priest

SENIOR LINE

George*
(1780–1843)

Sir John Lawson, 5th Bt*
(1744–1811)

Thomas Strickland Standish = (1) Anastasia Lawson (1769–1807)
(1763–1813) m. 1789
of Sizergh, Standish and Borwick (2) Catherine Gerard (d. 1862)
added surname and arms of Standish 1807

Cdr Walter Strickland* = Louisa Bonici of Malta (1833–1907)
(1824–67) 5th son m. 1858 heiress of Sir Nicholas Scebberas, 5th Count della
Catena, and the Bologna estates, Malta

= (2) Roger de
Montesquiou
comte de
Fezensac

Henriette de = (1) J. C. Matthiessen
Sercey* (2) Baron Henri de
(b. 1773) Finguerlin

Emma = Charles Standish
(1802–31) of Standish
m. 1822 ceased use of arms and
Strickland surname 1813

(1) Thomas = Gasparine
Strickland* de Finguerlin*
(1792–1835) (1805–46)
of Sizergh and
Borwick m. 1824

Walter Charles Strickland (1825–1903) = Rosetta Medex
sold Borwick 1854, settled Sizergh on his 2nd cousin 1896 (d. 1884) m. 1867

male line died out 1920

Lt-Cdr Thomas Hornyold-Strickland* of Sizergh, = Angela Engleheart*
7th Count della Catena 1940 (1921–83) (b. 1928) m. 1951

Henry Hornyold-Strickland of Sizergh = Claudine Poumirau
8th Count della Catena 1983 (b. 1951) m. 1979

Hugo (b. 1979) Thomas (b. 1985)

Roger Strickland = Annie Rowley
(1872–1938) (d. 1948) m. 1897

2 daus.

THE STRICKLAND FAMILY

THE MIDDLE AGES

Sizergh has been the home of the Strickland family for 700 years. The family is probably of Norman descent and originally lived at Castle Carrock, east of Carlisle. From the late 12th century it held lands at Great Strickland near Penrith, and Sizergh was acquired after the marriage in 1239 of Sir William de Stirkeland to Elizabeth Deincourt, the heiress of the Deincourt family, which had owned Sizergh since the 1170s.

The family name was originally 'Stirkeland' (the pastureland of young cattle or 'stirks'), and the family continued to be called 'de Stirkeland' for over a century after Sizergh had become its principal home. The family name evolved to 'Strykeland' and eventually, by 1385, to its modern form of 'Strickland'.

The first member of the family to make Sizergh his principal seat was Sir Walter de Stirkeland (d. c.1343) and it was probably his son, Sir Thomas (d. 1376), who built the tower. Its west façade still shows, beneath the top-storey window, the arms of Sir Walter's mother Elizabeth Deincourt quartered with those of Strickland (three silver shells on a black background) and taking precedence over them in the first quarter of the shield. Above this is the Strickland crest, a faggot of holly, which may derive from the family's association with the lucrative cattle-droving trade in Westmorland, where holly was cultivated at drove stopovers to provide valuable winter feed for the cattle.

The earliest substantial house at Sizergh is likely to have been built about 1310. It consisted of a great hall with open-timbered roof, central hearth, and front and rear entrances creating a cross-passage, or screens passage, at its north end where there was an attached service block. At the other end, there would have been a tower or a wing for the family apartments. It was this part which Sir Thomas rebuilt in the mid-14th century as a massive, four-storey tower containing the main family room – the solar – on the first floor. The solar was reached by a staircase wing off the back of the hall, and had exclusive access via a spiral stair to the bedchambers above and the vaulted basement below. On the south side, a large turret was designed to rear above the main battlemented parapet, adding a touch of swagger to a building that was clearly meant to show off the rising fortunes of the Stricklands.

Sir Walter de Stirkeland served with distinction in the Scottish wars of Edward I and Edward II and also regularly represented Westmorland in Parliament from 1307 to 1332. In 1307 he was rewarded by Edward I for his military service with a charter of free warren, giving him sole right to kill game on all his lands. In 1336 a further grant from Edward III authorised him to enclose the woods and lands at Sizergh to make a park. Possession of a park exempted the grantee from the Forest Laws and gave him full rights over the deer and other game there. Sizergh remained an enclosed park stocked with game until the 18th century.

By the time of Sir Walter's death about 1343, the Strickland family had become one of the most important in Westmorland. His direct descendants, alternately named Thomas and Walter and noted for their longevity, continued to represent the county in Parliament. They served Edward III and Henry V in the Hundred Years War in France, and Sir Thomas (d. 1455) had the honour of carrying the Banner of St George, the premier banner of England, at the battle of Agincourt in 1415. In

(Right) The mid-14th-century tower displays the arms of Deincourt and Strickland

Sizergh is famous for its richly carved overmantels, which were installed between 1563 and 1575. This example is in the Old Dining Room

1431 the same Sir Thomas also received a special licence from Pope Eugenius IV authorising him to have a portable altar at Sizergh.

Sir Thomas's son, Walter (*c.*1412–*c.*1467), was the only head of the family not to be knighted in the medieval period. During the Wars of the Roses he sided with the House of York, as did his son Sir Thomas (d. *c.*1497), who fought for Edward IV at the battle of Tewkesbury in 1471 and was knighted on the battlefield.

THE TUDOR PERIOD

The eventual victory of the Tudors had no adverse effects on the family's fortunes. On the contrary, the 16th century was without doubt the period when the Stricklands were at their most prosperous. Sir Thomas's son, Walter (d. 1506), was created a Knight of the Bath by Henry VII on the marriage of Prince Arthur and Catherine of Aragon in 1501. Sir Walter's son and grandson, both also called Walter – thus breaking with the tradition of alternating the names Walter and Thomas – fought in the Scottish wars of 1523 and 1542–5. As an indication of the family's growing prosperity we can note that the Stricklands were able to raise more men from their own estates than any other family in Westmorland for the Scottish war of the early 1540s.

The Stricklands benefited from two favourable marriages. Sir Thomas (d. *c.*1497) married, in 1464, Agnes Parr, the sister of Sir William Parr of Kendal Castle. Although the Parr family moved south to Northamptonshire after 1487, the family link was maintained and the Stricklands thereby obtained powerful friends at Court. Sir William Parr's granddaughter Catherine married Henry VIII in 1543 and his grandson became Marquess of

Northampton in 1547. It was Queen Catherine who was entrusted with the upbringing of the future Elizabeth I.

The other important marriage took place in 1515 between Sir Walter (1497–1528) and Katherine Neville. By this union the Stricklands acquired an important 1,200-acre (486ha) estate at Thornton Bridge in Yorkshire. The estate remained with the Stricklands of Sizergh until 1682 and for much of the 17th century even became the family's principal seat. Possession of lands in Yorkshire as well as Westmorland considerably enhanced the standing and wealth of the family, and facilitated both the important building works carried out at Sizergh during the late 1550s and 1560s and the exceptionally fine carved interior decorations produced from about 1558 to the mid-1580s.

The house was tripled in size within about seven years, creating an impressive first-floor hall over the medieval one, six new rooms over the service block, and two wings for a long gallery and domestic quarters. No record survives to identify the carvers responsible for the high quality of the interior. They also made oak chests, chairs and

forms for the new apartments before moving on to nearby Levens Hall in the 1580s.

The building works and interior decorations at Sizergh were started by Walter Strickland (1516–69) and his second wife Alice (d. 1588), who was praised for 'the integrity of her conduct and uprightness of heart'. They were not yet finished when Walter died, but were continued by his widow. About 1573 she married Thomas Boynton of Barmston (Yorkshire), who lived with her at Sizergh until his death in 1581 and helped her bring up Walter's young son Thomas Strickland (1564–1612). The Boyntons commissioned the decoration of the Boynton Room (dated 1575) and the magnificent Inlaid Chamber, which is contemporary with the inlaid great chamber at Gilling Castle in Yorkshire, made for Boynton's brother-in-law by his first marriage, Sir William Fairfax.

As a young man in 1536 Walter Strickland (1516–69) had been drawn unwillingly into the Pilgrimage of Grace by those leading this rebellion against Henry VIII's government, along with other Westmorland gentlemen, but he had been pardoned by the King. Thereafter, he seems to have

This extremely rare oak bench in the Banqueting Hall is one of a set made in 1562 for Walter Strickland

outwardly conformed to the religious changes during the reigns of Edward VI, Mary I and Elizabeth I. In 1564 he was described by the Bishop of Carlisle as 'of good Relligion', which doubtless helped to preserve the family's prosperity.

THE STUART PERIOD

Walter's son Thomas (1564–1612) represented Westmorland in the last Parliament of Elizabeth I (1601) and the first of James I (1604–11), and was created a Knight of the Bath by the new Stuart king at the coronation in July 1603. He also served as High Sheriff of Yorkshire and as a member of the Council of the North. The family's prospects at the start of the Stuart period seemed therefore to have been even better than they had been under the Tudors. In fact, the Stricklands were about to enter a period of serious financial decline, and it was Sir Thomas who was mainly responsible for this. He spent much of his time in London and

Sir Thomas Strickland (1564–1612), who gambled away much of his inheritance; English school, 1600 (Upper Hall)

impoverished the family estates by gambling, which, as his grandson warned, 'reduseth men to necessity, provokes swearing and cursing, the awthor of quarrells, makes men Steal, and torne robers'. He also married a Catholic, Margaret Curwen. His relatively early death in 1612 left her to bring up their seven children as Catholics, a fact that was to have a decisive effect on the future history of the family. From the beginning of the 17th century the Stricklands were to suffer the penalties and disadvantages of recusancy.

From Sir Thomas and his wife Margaret the two main Strickland families are descended. Their eldest son Robert, aged twelve, inherited the estates at Sizergh and Thornton Bridge. Their third son Walter married Anne Croft of Catterick (Yorkshire). Walter's children eventually inherited the Catterick lands and thus founded a new branch of the family.

Robert Strickland (1600–71) was an active supporter of Charles I during the crisis in the middle of the 17th century. He joined the King's army against the Scots in the Second Bishops' War of 1640 and was knighted at York the following year. When the Civil War started in 1642, he commanded a regiment in the Royalist army and he was probably present at the Royalist defeat at Marston Moor in 1644. His eldest son Thomas (1621–94) fought at Edgehill in 1642, was made a Knight Banneret, and served as a Lieutenant-Colonel until he was captured (and released) by the Parliamentarians in 1644. The family now paid the penalty of being both Catholic and Royalist. To avoid losing his lands, Sir Robert made over all his Westmorland and Yorkshire estates to his son Sir Thomas on the latter's first marriage in 1646. The lands were not sequestered, but the family had to pay very heavy fines. These, on top of the heavy gambling debts incurred by Sir Robert's father, brought the family finances to a low ebb. When the second Civil War broke out in 1648, both Sir Robert and Sir Thomas rejoined the King, and this time their estates were confiscated as a result. They were recovered only after paying another huge fine.

By his wife Jane (née Mosely), a widow whom he had married in 1646, Sir Thomas had obtained

Sir Robert Strickland (1600–71), who supported Charles I during the Civil War; by the anonymous painter 'JH' (Drawing Room)

both money and credit, enough to settle good marriage portions on his two daughters Alice and Jane. But he had no surviving son. When his wife died in 1671, he therefore decided to give Sizergh to his younger brother Walter, at that time Mayor of Ripon and married to Barbara Bellasis (sister of Lord Fauconberg). This brother had a daughter, and it was hoped that he would soon have a son to carry on the Strickland line at Sizergh. Unfortunately, Walter died almost immediately after this arrangement had been made, and as a result Sir Thomas found himself obliged to pay heavily to regain possession of what had been his own property. He also decided to remarry, in the now desperate hope of having a son who could inherit Sizergh. His second wife, whom he married in 1674, was Winifred Trentham. Her father Sir Christopher had only the life-use of the estate he occupied at Rocester Priory (Stafford-shire), and she brought no large dowry. By 1682 his second marriage had provided Sir Thomas with

not one but five sons, but with little to alleviate his financial problems.

The heavy debts incurred before and during the Civil Wars had already obliged Sir Thomas to go to Court to supplement his income, but this only made matters worse, according to the antiquary Thomas Machell, who noted that 'southeran life will not well suite with a Northern Estate; for they are generally more open-hearted than any other countery men'. He had been elected MP for the county of Westmorland in the Cavalier Parliament of 1661 and he remained a member until he was excluded from the House of Commons because of his Catholicism in March 1677. For a short while he had also served as a Commissioner of the Privy Seal (1669–70). Sir Thomas had meanwhile bought a lease of the duties on imported salt, but his speculation went badly wrong and he now incurred a very substantial loss. In 1682, when he finally gave up the lease, he was also obliged to sell his estate at Thornton Bridge. It was in these difficult circum-

Sir Thomas Strickland (1621–94), who followed James II into exile in France; attributed to Jacob Huysmans (Drawing Room)

James II; French school, after Sir Godfrey Kneller (Dining Room)

Robert Strickland, Rear-Admiral Sir Roger Strickland, had served with James II when he had been Lord High Admiral and was promoted to the rank of Vice-Admiral in 1687. It was these connections and the family's Catholicism that brought Sir Thomas and Lady Strickland to the attention of the King and Queen. In June 1688 Lady Strickland was present at the birth of the Prince of Wales and was appointed to be the child's Under-Governess. In the following month Sir Thomas was sworn in as a member of the Privy Council. The family's fortunes seemed at last to have turned.

By 1688, however, James II's policy of toleration and political equality for Catholics and Dissenters had made him unpopular with a large number of people. The birth of the Catholic Prince of Wales prompted the invasion of William of Orange. The result was the 'Glorious Revolution', which deposed James II and replaced him with William and Mary. One event which

stances that Sir Thomas and Lady Strickland began to see the patronage of the future James II as their best hope of salvation.

James was the younger brother and heir of Charles II, who had no legitimate children. As Duke of York, James had converted to Catholicism and married an Italian princess, Mary of Modena, in 1673. Mounting anti-Catholicism resulted in the Popish Plot scare of 1678–9, during which Sizergh, like other Catholic houses, was searched for weapons, but the attempt in 1679–81 to exclude the Duke of York from the succession, on the grounds that he was a Catholic, failed, and as a result James II succeeded his brother in 1685. Neither Sir Thomas nor Lady Strickland was a member of the households of the new King and Queen, but they were very well connected. In particular Sir Thomas's first cousin, Robert Strickland of Catterick, was appointed Vice-Chamberlain to the new Queen in 1685. Robert's wife Bridget was one of the Queen's Bedchamber Women. Moreover, the younger brother of

James II's queen, Mary of Modena, from whom the Stricklands acquired many of the Stuart relics at Sizergh; attributed to Alexis-Simon Belle after ?François de Troy (Dining Room)

contributed to the fall of James II was his decision to send the Queen and baby Prince to France for safety. On the night of 9–10 December 1688 Lady Strickland and a few other faithful servants secretly left Whitehall Palace and accompanied the Queen and Prince from Gravesend to Calais. After one unsuccessful attempt to follow them the next day, James II succeeded in making good his own escape and joined them in France soon after.

THE JACOBITE EXILE

The King and Queen were lent the château of Saint-Germain-en-Laye by Louis XIV as a temporary home, pending their restoration. The château is to the west of Paris and had been Louis' own principal residence before moving to Versailles in 1682. It enjoyed spectacular views towards Paris and was magnificently furnished. The King's supporters, soon known as Jacobites, began to assemble at Saint-Germain at the beginning of 1689. They included Sir Thomas Strickland and all the Stricklands of Catterick, together with Lady Strickland's relations from Biddulph Old Hall in Staffordshire, and various relations and friends from Westmorland and Lancashire. As hopes of an early restoration faded, it was in this expatriate community that Sir Thomas and Lady Strickland and their family were now destined to live.

At Saint-Germain Lady Strickland was in the second rank of the servants surrounding the Queen. The most important were the Ladies of the Bedchamber and the Governess of the Prince of Wales, who were the wives and daughters of peers. After them came the Bedchamber Women and the Under-Governess, who were the wives and daughters of gentlemen. Supervising the upbringing of the Prince, however, gave Lady Strickland a more generous salary than her equals and a spacious apartment on the principal floor of the château with the royal family and the Governess. From the spring of 1691, Lady Strickland served as acting Governess, until she was replaced by the Countess of Erroll. But Sir Thomas, although a Privy Councillor, had no active employment at the Court and was suffering

Robert Strickland recorded the salaries and pensions awarded to members of the exiled court at Saint-Germain in this ledger

from ill-health, so in October 1692 the Queen allowed Lady Strickland to hand over her post of Under-Governess to someone else and retire with him to an English convent of Poor Clares at Rouen, where her half-brother happened to be the chaplain.

Lady Strickland was away from Saint-Germain until January 1694, when Sir Thomas died at Rouen. As Lady Erroll had also died shortly before, Lady Strickland was given the exceptional honour of being appointed Governess of the Prince for the remaining period of a year and a half, before his education was entrusted to a Governor at the age of seven in June 1695. A portrait of the prince in armour in 1694–5, but with the head clearly modelled on an earlier portrait of 1691, when Lady Strickland had been acting Governess, was later commissioned to commemorate this important appointment; the picture hangs in the Dining Room.

By 1695 Lady Strickland had to look after her own children and their inheritance. Before leaving for France, Sir Thomas had wisely taken two important precautions to ensure that his property would not be seized by William and Mary's new government. At the end of 1688 he had placed

*Lady Strickland acted as Governess to the young
'James III'; attributed to J. van Schuppen (Dining Room)*

*Winifred, Lady Strickland (1645–1725), who carefully
preserved the Sizergh estates during the family's long
exile; by William Wissing (Drawing Room)*

Sizergh in trust with two family servants. He had
also arranged for three of his four surviving sons
(Walter, Roger and Thomas) to join him in France
at the beginning of 1689 with official passes from
the new government. (The other son, Robert, was
left in England with a member of the family.)
Possession of these passes meant that they could
safely return to England at a later date. In 1696 the
Jacobite estates were confiscated by the government in London, but Sizergh remained securely in
trust. In 1699, when England and France were
again at peace, Sir Thomas's eldest son Walter,
who had been a Groom of the Bedchamber to the
Prince, was able to return to England to claim his
inheritance.

Lady Strickland, a woman of great courage, had
already gone to England in the autumn of 1695 to
prepare the way. She seems to have remained in
England for about four and a half years, to ensure

*(Right) Walter Strickland (1675–1715), who modernised
the great hall; English school, c.1700 (Drawing Room)*

(Above and right) Roger Strickland (1680–1704) and his brother, Thomas (c.1682–1740), who became Bishop of Namur; by Belle (Upper Hall)

that the family's interests were safeguarded. She had connections at Gray's Inn, where she placed her son Robert as a student, and in 1697 she began legal action there to recover Sizergh. Before returning to Saint-Germain in 1700, she had not only succeeded in her aim, but had also consolidated the family finances, to ensure that Walter Strickland could afford to maintain Sizergh properly. Walter was thus able to modernise the 16th-century great hall by giving it a central entrance reached by an external staircase, in the fashionable Baroque idiom he had come across at Saint-Germain. Her sons Roger and Thomas were persuaded to hand over their inheritance to their eldest brother, to remain in France and make what careers they could there. In a deed of December 1699 Lady Strickland also gave everything she possessed in England, except for a small annuity, to her eldest son.

Lady Strickland left the country for the last time in the spring of 1700, when Walter Strickland married Anne Salvin of Croxdale (County Durham), the daughter of an old family friend. At Saint-Germain, she was appointed by the Queen to be a Bedchamber Woman. Shortly after her return Lady Strickland commissioned the Jacobite Court painter Alexis-Simon Belle to produce portraits of the two sons who had remained with her in France. They can be seen today at Sizergh and were probably painted in 1703, before the early death of Roger (1680–1704) and after Thomas (c.1682–1740) had begun to train for the priesthood at the English Seminary in Paris. Thomas caused his mother great grief by eventually deserting the Jacobite cause and supporting the Hanoverian succession after 1714. When the French government had also turned against the Jacobites, he was rewarded with a wealthy abbey in Normandy, and in 1727 became Bishop of Namur in the Austrian Netherlands.

Between 1700 and 1718 Lady Strickland acquired the Stuart portraits and other relics which are such an important part of the collection at Sizergh today. It is not clear when and how she obtained them. Some porcelain was almost certainly given to her after the Queen's death in 1718, when the Bedchamber Women received her personal possessions. The paintings, however, must have been acquired earlier, because none of the Queen's pictures was given away to the Bedchamber Women at that time. The most likely explanation is that they were given or promised to Lady Strickland by Mary of Modena before she died.

In September 1701, shortly after Lady Strickland had returned from England, James II died at Saint-Germain. Much of Catholic Europe immediately recognised the Prince of Wales as the new *de jure* King James III. A war with France from 1702 to 1713 (the War of the Spanish Succession) prevented any contact between the two halves of the family in England and France. Visits were resumed in 1713, when Thomas went to Sizergh

and Walter brought his children to be educated in France. Walter fell ill while visiting his daughter Mary at the English convent of Poor Clares at Rouen and died in October 1715, leaving Sizergh to his fourteen-year-old son, Thomas Peter (1701–54).

Lady Strickland retired from Saint-Germain in June 1718, after the death of the Queen, and passed the remaining years of her life with her half-brother at the convent in Rouen where her husband and eldest son lay buried. The deaths of all but her youngest son, by then a wealthy abbot who had deserted the Jacobite cause, influenced her when she came to make her will, shortly before her own death in April 1725. Apart from various specific legacies, she left all her French furniture and household goods to a servant, so they never returned to Sizergh, apart from the scagliola table. But all her pictures, her plate and her porcelain were left to her grandson Thomas Peter.

This Japanese Imari tureen with silver mounts dating from 1717–18 was given to the family by Mary of Modena

(Above and right) Thomas Peter Strickland (1701–54) and his wife, Mary (1702–38); painted by an unknown artist c.1735 (Upper Hall)

THE GEORGIAN AND VICTORIAN PERIODS

During the rest of the 18th century the Stricklands of Sizergh maintained their Jacobite loyalty, as is shown most notably by the presence in the Dining Room of a fine gilt plaster bust of Prince Charles Edward Stuart (James III's elder son, known as 'Bonnie Prince Charlie'). But the head of the family now remained in England and made no attempt to join the Court of James III. The exiled King, known to his enemies as the 'Pretender', had left France and settled in Rome. Nevertheless strong links were maintained with the Court through their cousins, the Stricklands of Catterick, particularly when Thomas Peter Strickland of Sizergh and Roger, the head of the Catterick branch, married two sisters, daughters of Simon Scrope of Danby-on-Ure (Yorkshire), in 1728 and 1726 respectively. Roger's brother, Francis (1691–1746), joined the Stuart Court in Rome in

Thomas Peter and Mary Strickland's eldest son, Walter (1729–61); by George Romney (Drawing Room)

1734, becoming a close friend of Prince Charles Edward, and he was one of the seven men with him at Moidart, when the Prince launched the 1745 rebellion in Scotland. He was with the Jacobite army when it marched through Kendal on its advance to Derby at the end of that year, but fell ill and died as the Prince's army retreated back to Scotland.

Thomas Peter Strickland began to modify Sizergh, introducing several Neo-classical interiors, Venetian windows and Georgian sash-windows. He and his wife Mary had three sons who survived into manhood. The eldest, Walter (1729–61), inherited Sizergh but died young without children. The second, William (1731–1819), became a distinguished Jesuit priest. The third, Charles (1734–70), also inherited Sizergh and had four children before he too died young. The brothers were among the earliest patrons of George

Romney, who painted them and their two wives in 1760 and 1762.

In 1762 Charles married Cecilia Towneley (1741–1814), the heiress of important estates at Standish (near Wigan) and Borwick (near Carnforth) in Lancashire. Cecilia, following the death of Charles, transformed the central portion of Sizergh into a modern country house in 1773–4 by taking down the first-floor hall and putting up a Neo-classical saloon (the present Drawing Room) with attic storey and neo-Gothic exterior. Her architect was John Hird of Cartmel, who also replaced the Baroque external staircase with a double flight of steps to a new front door in a realigned outer wall, making the space behind into a vestibule, now the Upper Hall. Cecilia's second husband, whom she married in 1779, was Jarrard Strickland (1741–95), a first cousin of her first husband Charles. In old age, rheumatism

Thomas Strickland (1792–1835); by John Ferneley, 1819 (Stone Parlour)

The garden front in 1822; engraving by Higham after Buckler

confined her to a wheelchair, but she had her carriage specially adapted to take it.

Cecilia Strickland had several children by each of her two husbands, and these two families are referred to as the senior and the junior lines. The senior line continued to own Sizergh until 1896, when it was re-entailed on the junior line.

Cecilia's eldest son Thomas, who had owned Sizergh since 1770, also inherited both Standish and Borwick in 1807. When he died in 1813, he divided his property between his two sons. Charles, the older (1790–1863), was given Standish and changed his name from Strickland to Standish. Thomas, the younger (1792–1835), was given both Sizergh and Borwick. One unfortunate result of this division was that some of the contents of Sizergh were given to the older brother and transferred to Standish Hall, which was eventually sold in 1922.

The two brothers married half-sisters, the great-nieces of Madame de Genlis, mistress of Philippe 'Egalité', the father of King Louis-Philippe of France. This was to be important because they both decided to live in France, thus beginning what was in effect a second period of exile for the Strickland family. The son and grandson of Charles Standish both married into well-known French aristocratic families. When the line died out in 1920, the estate and all its contents were left to Matilde de Montesquiou-Fezensac, who was married to Charles Widor, the composer and organist of the church of Saint-Sulpice in Paris. Everything, including the items originally from Sizergh, was sold in 1922.

When Thomas Strickland of Sizergh and Borwick died in 1835, the two estates passed to his son Walter, then only ten years old. His mother Gasparine (née de Finguerlin) married Roger de Montesquiou, comte de Fezensac, and Sizergh was let out to tenants while Walter remained in France. In 1854 he sold Borwick Hall and brought

Lady Edeline Strickland (1870–1918); by Giuseppe Calì (Upper Hall)

was the Stuart silver gilt toilet service, which had belonged to Lady Strickland at Saint-Germain and been bequeathed by her to her grandson back in 1725. This was sold, however, when Walter died in 1903. (It is now in the new Silver Gallery in the Victoria and Albert Museum.)

The fact that Sizergh and most of its contents have remained together, to be visited and enjoyed today, was almost entirely due to Walter's cousin Sir Gerald Strickland, the head of the junior line of the family and, like Walter himself, a great-grandson of Cecilia (née Towneley).

Sir Gerald, Lord Strickland (1861–1940); by Edward Caruana Dingli (Passage)

some of its fine oak panelling to Sizergh. (It is now in the Bindloss Room.) Despite this sale, Walter Strickland experienced financial problems. In 1891 he sold to the Victoria and Albert Museum the panelling of the Inlaid Chamber, followed by the state bed and stained glass in 1896. In the same year, furniture, tapestries and pictures were put up for auction at Christie's, although fortunately much was recovered. The most important loss was a large portrait of James III by Belle, painted in 1712 as a companion to that of his sister Princess Louise-Marie (c.1710) and in an identical frame. (It now belongs to the Government Art Collection.) One item of importance which Walter retained

Mary and Henry Hornyold-Strickland, who donated Sizergh to the National Trust in 1950; by Edward Caruana Dingli (Old Dining Room)

THE LAST HUNDRED YEARS

Gerald's father Walter had been a Commander in the Royal Navy, helping to suppress the slave trade off Africa. He was also a skilful conjuror: when asked why he did not play cards, he proceeded to deal himself all the trumps. He had married into an important Maltese family: his wife was Louisa Bonici, heiress of the 5th Count della Catena, a title which could be passed down through the female line. Gerald Strickland had inherited the title as 6th Count della Catena in 1875, and since 1889 had served as Chief Secretary to the Governor of Malta. An agreement was made between him and his cousin Walter that he would become the new owner of Sizergh, and thus keep the property in the Strickland family, in return for relieving Walter of all his debts. Sizergh now received the collected · possessions of the junior line, including various family portraits which had belonged to Lady Strickland at Saint-Germain.

In 1897 the new owner of Sizergh was created a Knight of the Order of St Michael and St George. Sir Gerald was married to Lady Edeline Sackville (1870–1918), a daughter of the 7th Earl De La Warr. Three of their first six children were born at Sizergh, which they visited as much as Sir Gerald's duties in Malta would allow. From 1902 until 1917, however, Sir Gerald served as Colonial Governor, successively, of the Leeward Islands, Tasmania, Western Australia and New South Wales. Apart from an extended visit in 1908, between two of these postings, the house was mainly closed during those years.

Sir Gerald and Lady Strickland had two more children after he had become Colonial Governor, but of a total of eight children only five survived, all of them girls. It was not until May 1919, by which time Lady Strickland had died in Malta, that Sir Gerald was finally able to return to Sizergh with his daughters and open up the house. Thereafter, he spent the summer months in England and the rest of the year in Malta.

Lt-Cdr and Mrs Thomas Hornyold-Strickland by Edward Carvana Dingli and Ronald Dickinson (Upper Hall)

Sir Gerald Strickland had an important political career in both Malta and England. He was a member of the Maltese Legislative Assembly and, after the establishment of self-government in 1921, leader of the opposition. He was Prime Minister of a coalition government from 1927 to 1932 and later founded the influential *Times of Malta* to resist the growing influence of Italian Fascism on the island. In England, meanwhile, he stood successfully as the Conservative candidate for Lancaster in the General Election of November 1924 and remained an MP until he was given a peerage as Baron Strickland of Sizergh in 1928. Shortly before he died in 1940, after Italy and Great Britain had gone to war, he had once again been returned to head the Maltese government.

It was Lord Strickland who gave to Sizergh its present-day appearance, by commissioning the Kendal architect J. F. Curwen to replace the external staircase with a carriageway driven through the centre of the house. His final legacy to Sizergh was the creation of the new gardens in 1926–8, following his marriage to Margaret Hulton, sister of the publisher Sir Edward Hulton, Bt, and together they supervised the making of one of the most beautiful and imaginative gardens in the north of England.

In 1931 Lord Strickland settled the estate upon his eldest daughter Mary and her husband Henry Hornyold, who took the name Hornyold-Strickland. It was thanks to them, and their son Lieutenant-Commander Thomas Hornyold-Strickland, that the house and contents and other adjoining lands were donated to the National Trust in 1950. The latter's widow, Mrs Thomas Hornyold-Strickland, still lives at Sizergh.